T0380663

COOKING *with* MRS. FAYE

BRENDA RUSLEY REESE

AuthorHouse™
1663 Liberty Drive
Bloomington, IN 47403
www.authorhouse.com
Phone: 1 (800) 839-8640

Because of the dynamic nature of the Internet, any web addresses or links contained in this book may have changed since publication and may no longer be valid. The views expressed in this work are solely those of the author and do not necessarily reflect the views of the publisher, and the publisher hereby disclaims any responsibility for them.

History on southern cooking https://en.m.wikipedia.org/wiki/SoulfoodFollow

Any people depicted in stock imagery provided by Getty Images are models, and such images are being used for illustrative purposes only.
Certain stock imagery © Getty Images.

This book is printed on acid-free paper.

ISBN: 978-1-7283-5893-2 (sc)
ISBN: 978-1-7283-5895-6 (hc)
ISBN: 978-1-7283-5894-9 (e)

Print information available on the last page.

Published by AuthorHouse 04/16/2020

author**HOUSE**®

COOKING *with* MRS. FAYE

FEATURING QUANETTA RAY

Quanetta Ray is one of Mrs. Reese' grandchildren, and is continuing the tradition of southern cooking as the 6th generation. At the age of six, Quanetta start cooking and helping her grandmother in the kitchen. Falling in love with the smell of the different foods, she decided to enroll in the prestigious institution of Johnson & Wales University to pursue her Bachelors Degree in Culinary Arts. Upon attaining her degree, her dream is to open her own food truck. As a devoted and driven young woman, her grandmother has no doubt that she will be successful and showing the world what Chef Ray has to offer.

HISTORY ON SOUL FOOD

"Soul food was originated back during slavery. The masters would give the undesirable parts of animals the scraps of vegetables' that the masters didn't want like collard greens and kale. After awhile, certain recipes that were prepared often and cooking techniques had to be passed down orally because it was illegal in many states for slaves to learn to read or write. Many years later, the first known soul food cook was by Abby Fisher, entitled *What Mrs. Fisher Knows About Old Southern Cooking* and published in 1881".

SOUL FOOD AND MY FAMILY

My grandmother and her friends worked in the cafeteria at a local trade school. When they got together for their quilting circle, they would eat teacakes and talk about ideas and trade recipes to try out. They would try it out as a featured item at home and if it got good reviews then it stayed. My grand mother never wrote her recipes down, but she taught her daughters, how to cook who then shared the cooking experience with me. When I got old enough to reach the stove, they both helped cultivate my desire to stay a part of the kitchen. I in turn taught my kids and my grandchildren. I have decided to share these recipes with those who want them.

CONTENTS

Side Dishes

Pies, Breads, Cakes

Salads

Oven Baked Ham with Pineapple and Cherries

Ingredient (100% homemade)

Ingredients: 3 to 5 pound Picnic Ham, 1 can of sliced pineapples, 1 can of pitted, stemless can cherries, 6 tooth picks, brown sugar (optional).

STEP 1:

Place the ham in a medium to large pan. Pin the pineapples and cherries to the ham with the toothpicks, placing the cherries inside of the circles of the pineapples.

(Optional): Carefully rub the brown sugar all over the surface of the ham.

STEP 2:

Add the juice from the pineapples and a 1/3 cup of water into the bottom of the pan. Cover with aluminum foil and cook in the oven for 1 ½ to 2 hour on 300 degrees Fahrenheit, checking in every 30 TO 45 minutes to basted the ham in the juices to keep it moist.

Salmon Croquettes

Ingredients (95% homemade use canned salmon)

Ingredients: 1 (10-ounce) can pink salmon, 1 small onion, diced, 1 large egg, ½ cup of self rising flour and corn meal mix the both.

1/2 teaspoon salt 1/2 teaspoon freshly ground black pepper.

STEP 1:

In a skillet, add 1-cup vegetable oil on medium-high heat

STEP 2:

Remove and throw out the thebones in the middle of the salmon, place salmon in the mixing bowl and stir in the onion, egg, 4 tablespoons for flour, salt, and pepper. (If the mixture is too moist, add more cornmeal/flour mix).

On a separate plate, create a mixture of flour and cornmeal.

STEP 3:

Spoon (use a tablespoon) a small portions of the salmon mixture in a ball and flatten into ¼-inch thick disks. Coat the disks in the flour mixture and, place in hot oil. Brown on both sides, remove, and drain on paper towel. Serve hot with rice (optional).

Chicken and Dumplings

Ingredient (95 % homemade)

3 pounds of chicken breast, 2 pack of Annie dumpling, 1 teaspoon of garlic powder,1 teaspoon of black pepper, 1 pinch of salt,1/2 slice onions., and 1 chicken bouillon cube.

STEP 1:

In a 3 quart pot add 2 ½ cup of water cook on medium high combine garlic black pepper and chicken bouillon cubes.

STEP 2:

Wash and add cleaned chicken breast on a plate add dry ingredient mixture on both side of the chicken. Put season chicken in pot with water Cover and cook for 45 minutes to 1 hour. After chicken is cook thoroughly, remove from the pot and allow broth to simmer on medium-high heat for 10 minutes.

STEP 3:

Fold dumpling in half and place in boiling chicken both, stir general cook until tender, ½ slice onions (optional).

STEP 4:

Cut the cook chicken in 1-inch cubes and add to dumpling, cook on low heat for 10 minutes and serve hot

Southern Fried Chicken

Ingredient (100 % homemade) 1 whole chicken cut-up

2 teaspoon of garlic. 1 teaspoon of salt, pepper, 2 cup of flour, 1 egg, 1 cup of milk, 2 quart pot, 2 ½ cup of oil on medium high.

After cleaning and washing the chicken, put the oil in pot and cook on medium high. In a medium bowl add egg, and milk beat together. In a medium another bowl, add the self-rising flour once you add the salt, pepper, garlic, dip the chicken in the egg and milk basic then into the flour and into the hot oil.

Stick a fork in the chicken. If blood is still coming from it, then it not done.

Chicken Liver and Gizzards

Chicken Liver and Gizzard are cook the same way ingredient: (100% homemade)

1 POUND of liver or gizzards

(1 cup milk, 2 eggs if you want a crispy taste), 1 cup flour,

½ teaspoon of salt, ½ teaspoon of black pepper,

2 tablespoon of garlic powder, 2 cup of oil

In a skillet add the oil and let get hot. In another bowl add flour. In another bowl mix milk and eggs.

Clean the fat off the chicken liver or gizzards add salt and pepper, garlic powder dip one at a time in the flour then put into hot oil.

Cook for 7 to 10 minutes (take out of skillet and cut if no blood is running out then I they are done.

Fried Beef Liver

Ingredient: (100% homemade) 1 pound of beef liver, 1 teaspoon of salt and pepper, I teaspoon a garlic. ½ cup of self rising flour, 1 ½ cup of oil

STEP 1:

Add oil to skillet and put on medium high heat

STEP 2:

Wash and add all dry ingredient to liver on both side

STEP 3:

Cover liver with flour and put in hot oil cook on both side for 3 to 5 minutes.

Serve hot.

13

Chitterlings and Hog Maws

Ingredient: 100% homemade, 10 pound bucket of chitterlings and 5 pound of Hog Maws, 1 large onion cut in1/3 cubes half,1 teaspoon of salt and pepper. 1 teaspoon season salt,1/3 cup of 1/3 cup of apple cider vinegar, 2 tablespoon of garlic, 1/2 stick of butter, 1 teaspoon of Italian seasoning

STEP 1:

Clean the Chitterlings, pull the inside layer of the fat off and discard. The shinning, thick part is the chitterling. Do one by one until you have all the chitterlings clean. Cut in half, Put clean in bucket and place in warm water.

STEP 2:

Clean Hog Maws just pull the fat off of the hog maw which is call the lining and slice your hog maws in big cubes Soak your Chitterling and hog maws in salt water for ½ hour, rinse after the ½ hour and go to step 3.

STEP 3:

In a 4-quart pot, add 2 1/2 cups of hot water and all ingredient

Let cook on medium for 4 hours or until tender.

Serve with hot sauce.

Smoothed Beef Liver in a Creamy Onion Gravy

Ingredient: (100% homemade)

1 pound of beef liver, 1 whole onion slice, 1 teaspoon of salt and pepper, ½ cup of self rising flour1 1 ½ cup of oil, 1 teaspoon of garlic powder

STEP 1

In a skillet or pot, add oil turn on medium heat

STEP 2:

Wash liver and add salt, pepper, garlic. Batter both side in flour(use ½ of the cup) and add to oil in skillet cook on each side for 5 minutes

Remove liver (put on plate) and pour out 90% of oil. Add onions and cook for 3 minutes, then add 2 tablespoons of the flour. Mix well. Cook and stir for 2 minutes, then add 1 cup of water, stir well and cook for 3 to 5 more minutes. Then add liver and cook for 5 more minutes on medium heat. Reduce heat, place a lid on it, and continue to cook for 10 minutes. Make sure it don't stick, if dry add ½ cup of water.

BBQ Chicken

INGREDIENT: (100% homemade)

2 Whole Chickens cut up

2 Teaspoon of Garlic powder

2 bottle of BBQ sauce, 1 onion, ½ teaspoon of salt and pepper

STEP 1

Wash and clean excess fat off chicken

STEP 2:

Add garlic powder, salt, and pepper on both side of the chicken.

STEP 3:

Into the pan, add 1 cup of water put in oven for 30 minutes. Slice onion and add BBQ Sauce over the chicken cover the pan with foil for 15 minutes.

To check and make sure the chicken is done; take a piece of chicken out breaks open and look at the bone if no blood then it is done.

Bake/BBQ Chicken w/o skin in the Oven

INGREDIENT: (100% homemade)

1 Whole chicken cut-up (wash and cut fat from the chicken

1 Teaspoon of pepper and salt if desire

1 Teaspoon of garlic 1 Onion and ½ cup of water in the pan

STEP 1:

Season the chicken with garlic, pepper and salt on both side

STEP 2:

Place the chicken in a medium pan, spread all dark meat the legs and thighs together and the wings and breast together spread the raw onion all over the raw chicken. Put aluminum foil over the pan for 20 minutes. After 20 minutes, remove.

For BBQ just add 1 bottle of your favorite BBQ sauce and put back in oven for 15 minutes

Cook on 300 degrees in the oven.

Stuff Chicken Breast with Bacon and Turkey Slices

Ingredient: (100% homemade)

3 to 6 chicken breast with the bones,9 to 15 slice of turkey slice, 6 to 9 pieces of bacon cook, 1 tablespoon of garlic powder, ½ teaspoon of salt(optional) and pepper, ½ onions thin slice . ½ cup of shred cheddar cheese and ½ cup of Mozella cheese

STEP 1:

Clean the fat from the chicken and put in a pan add garlic powder, pepper and salt is optional put onions all over the chicken and put in oven for 20 minutes.

STEP 2:

Put uncook bacon in oven and let cook until Krispy, once done take out and use a plate wrap the bacon and shred cheeses into the turkey slice use several tooth picks to hold in place

STEP 3:

take chicken out and check to make sure it is done by separating (pull from the bone to see if there is blood then put back in oven if no blood then make a slice in the center of the chicken breast and add the wrap turkey slice . On top of the chicken add sweet and sour sauce and shred cheese, put in oven until the cheese melt serve hot

Fried Fatback

Ingredient: 8 slices of Fried Fatback and 1 medium baking pan

STEP 1:

Get 8 to 10 slices of fatback (white meat) wash the meat put in the baking pan and put in oven on 300 degrees for 10 minutes or until the skin (the top part of the meat) is crispy remove from oven let sit for 5 minutes

Can be serve with rice.

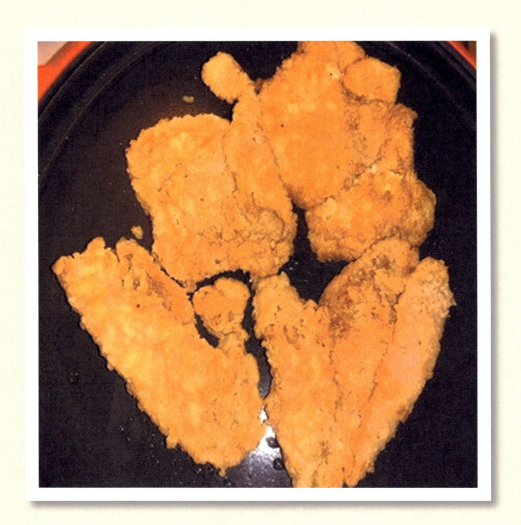

Deep Fried Chicken Skins

Ingredient (100% homemade)

Chicken skin, ½ teaspoon of salt (optional) ½ teaspoon of pepper,1 teaspoon of garlic powder,2 cup of cooking oil, ½ cup of self rising flour, 2 eggs, 1/3 cup of milk

STEP 1:

Mix and beat eggs and milk together

STEP 2:

Wash chicken skins add salt, pepper and garlic powder together mix well

STEP 3:

On a medium high put the oil in the skillet and let it get hot once hot

STEP 4:

Place season chicken in the egg batter then into the flour and place in hot oil cook until crisp

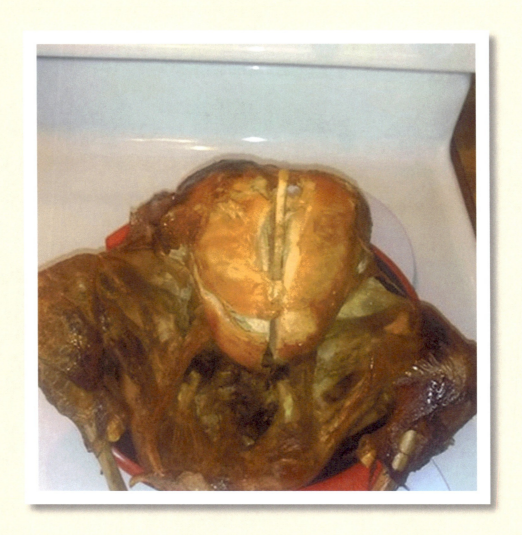

Whole Turkey

Ingredient: (100% homemade)

3 to 5 pound whole turkey, 1 onion, ½ cup of beer or wine, creole seasoning, 2 tablespoon of garlic powder, 2 cup of water

STEP 1:

Wash and get the chicken gizzard and liver from the inside of the whole turkey.

STEP 2:

Place turkey in a roasting pan. Use ½ the dry ingredient to rub all over the turkey and place the whole onion inside the turkey. Using a butter knife, punch several holes throughout the turkey and use the remaining of the seasoning mix with ½ beer or ½ cup of wine and place in each hole. Put in oven on 300 for 1 ½ hour if the pan is dry add 1 cup of water.

Oven cooked Turkey Wing with sweet Onions

Ingredient (100% homemade)

3 to 6 turkey wings, ½ onion, 1 teaspoon of garlic and herb, 1 teaspoon of creole seasoning, add 1 pinch of salt (optional) 12 pinches of black pepper, 1 ½ cup of water

STEP 1:

Wash and seasoning the turkey wings with the dry ingredients, put on a baking pan and add onions all over the turkey wings, add the water in pan and cook in the oven on 300 degrees for 45 minutes to 1 hour 15 minutes. (To check to see if done take 1 turkey wing out and use a folk go to the bone if no blood then it is done) serve hot.

Smoke Neck Bones

Ingredient: (100% homemade)

1 onion cut in cubes, ½ teaspoon of salt, 1//2 teaspoon of black pepper, 2 cups of hot water, 6 to 8 neckbones

In a 2-quart pot, add hot water, and the entire ingredients

Cook on medium for 45 minutes turn down fire to low add cover let cook for 20 more minutes the neck bones will be so tender they will fall off bones.

They can be serve with the following hot sauce, rice.

Smothered pork chops with Bone in a creamy onion gravy

Ingredient: (100% homemade)

6 porkchop that is ¼ inch thick, 1 large onion cut into medium cubes, 1 cup of flour.2 cup of cooking oil. 1 teaspoon of black pepper, 1 ½-teaspoon garlic powder,

STEP 1:

In a skillet, pour the oil n allow oil to get hot, (skillet on medium high).

STEP 2:

Wash the meat add salt,pepper, garlic powder .batter the pork chops with flour and put in hot oil cook until golden brown on each side.

STEP 3:

Once all the pork chops have cooked, remove from skillet and pour 90% of the oil out of skillet and add onions cubed, 2 tablespoon of flour a pinch of garlic, pepper and salt stir and add 1 ½ cup of water. Simmer for 5 to 7 minutes then add the cook pork chops cover and simmer for 10 to 15 minutes keep checking to make sure it is not sticking. Serve hot.

Fried Boneless Pork Chops

Ingredient (100% homemade)

One pack of boneless Porkchops /Porkchops with bones. 1 Cup of flour, 2 tablespoon of garlic, ½ teaspoon of salt (optional) and pepper, 2 cup of cooking oil

STEP 1:

In a 3-quart pot add the oil and turn the pot on medium high

STEP 2:

Wash and add pepper and garlic powder and salt if desire onto the pork chops (both side) dip season meat into the flour and place in hot oil cook until golden brown. Drain /place on dry paper towel on a plate and serve hot.

BBQ Pig Feet

Ingredient (100% homemade)

3-6 pig feet, 2 chop onion, 2 teaspoon of garlic, ½ cup of wine or beer 2 teaspoon of black pepper and 1 teaspoon of salt (optional) 2 cups of water 2 bottle of BBQ sauce

Wash pigs feet with warm water on both sides, add all ingredients. (Except the onions and BBQ sauce, they will be the last) Once in the pan, add sliced onion, add 2 cups of water and put in oven on 300 for 45 minute to an hour. (Cover with foil)

Once the pig feet start separating add the 2 bottle of BBQ sauce all over put back in oven for 20 minutes.(make sure the pan have water in the bottom of pan so that it will not burn or stick. You can always add more garlic and BBQ sauce. If it comes apart when you stick a folk in it, then it is done, if not add 1/3 cup of water and let cook for 30 more minutes.

Boiled Pig Feet with Sweet Onions

Ingredient 3-6 pig feet,

2 chop onion, 2 teaspoon of garlic,

2 teaspoon of black pepper and 1 teaspoon of salt (optional) 2 cups of water, 2 cap of wine

STEP 1:

Wash meat, and add dry seasons

STEP 2:

Put 3 cups of hot water and ½ of chop onions, 2 caps of wine in a 3 quart pot

STEP 3:

Allow to cook for 1 ½ hour If tender they will fall apart when you stick a folk in it if not add 1/3 cup of hot water and let it cook for addition 15 to 30 minutes.

BBQ Pig Tail with Onions

Ingredient (100% homemade)

3-5 pig TAIL, 2 chop onion, 2 teaspoon of garlic, 1 Bottle of BBQ Sauce 2 teaspoon of black pepper and 1 teaspoon of salt (optional) 1/2 cups of water 1/3 cup of soy sauce

STEP 1:

Wash and place meat in the pan.

STEP 2:

Put all of the dry ingredients over the meat. Place the onions all over the meat and put the water and soy sauce in the pan.

STEP 3:

Put in the oven on 350 degrees for 1 hour. After 30 minutes, add BBQ sauce. If pan is dry, add 1/3 cup of water in pan.

Baked Pig Tails with Sweet Onions

Ingredient (100% homemade)

3-5 pig TAIL, 2 chop onion, 2 teaspoon of garlic, 2 teaspoon of black pepper and 1 teaspoon of salt (optional) 1/2 cups of water 1/3 cup of soy sauce

Wash and place all ingredients on both side of the meat. Place in the pan, put onions all over the meat and put in the oven on 300 degrees for 1 hour. (Keep checking to make sure that there is water in bottom of pan.

Stew Meat in a Onion Brown Gravy

Ingredient: (100% homemade)

1 pound of stew meat, 1 onion slice. 2 tablespoon of self rising flour,1 teaspoon of salt and pepper and 1 teaspoon of Creole seasoning, 1 teaspoon of garlic and herb, ½ cup of water, and 3 tablespoon of cooking oil.

STEP 1:

Wash stew meat and place in the skillet add all of the dry season (1/2 of salt and pepper) add the water let cook on medium for 20 to 25 minutes, remove stew meat from fire, put in a plate or bowl

STEP 2:

In the same skillet while it is still hot add the cooking oil, flour, salt, and pepper, and then add the onions let cook for 10 minutes.

STEP 3:

Add the meat and cook on medium low for 30 minutes or until sauce thicken (if too think add water) Serve hot.

Willie's BBQ Baby Back Pork Ribs

Ingredient: (100% homemade)

2 Slabs cut into 1 bone, 2 tablespoon garlic,1/2 beer or a cup of wine, tenderizer, salt, pepper, 1 large onion, 2 cup of water in alumni pan.2 bottle of BBQ sauce.

In a large alumni pan wash and sprinkle all dry seasonal (1 tablespoon of garlic arrange raw meat in pan add onion and water place in oven for 45 minutes on 325 degrees.

In a mixing bowl, add 1 tablespoon of garlic the wine or beer, 2 bottle of BBQ sauce mix well and pour over meat and cook on 325 degree for 30 more minutes make sure the pan is not dry. if dry add water.

49

FISH and Cheezie Grits

INGREDIENT: (100% of homemade)

3 WHOLE TALIPIA FILLET

½ Teaspoon salt and pepper, ½ cup flour, ½ cup of corn meal ½ cup sharp shred cheese, ½ cup of grits,1 table spoon of garlic, 1 cup of oil in the skillet or pot (I prefer to fry fish in a 3 to 4 quart pot) 2 quart pot, 2 cups of hot water

STEP 1:

Put oil in pot and let get hot.

STEP 2:

In a quart pot, add 2 cups of hot water add a pinch of salt (optional)

STEP 3:

Mix the flour and corn meal together

STEP 4:

Wash fish, lay fish on a flat pan and add salt pepper and garlic put the flour/meal on both side of the fish

STEP 5:

Place each piece of fish in hot oil and let cook until golden

For the cheese grits

In the pot with hot water, add the ½ cup of girts cook on a medium (keep stirring to make sure they are not sticking after cooking for 10 minutes add the shred cheese with pepper and salt is optional. If the girts is not cheesy enough add more let cook for 10 more minutes on low.

Shrimp and Cheesy Grits

Ingredient: 100% homemade

1 pound of devein shrimps, ½ onion, 1 teaspoon of Creole seasoning,1 teaspoon of Garlic and herb seasoning, ½ stick of butter.

(For grits) in a 2 quart pot add 1 cup of water, 1 pinch of salt (optional) 1 pinch of pepper, ½ cup of girts,1 ½ cup of sharp shred cheese

STEP 1:

In the 2 quart pot add water and all ingredient for the girts cook on medium low for 15 minutes add 1 ½ cup of cheese, constantly stir

STEP 2:

For shrimps: in a skillet add wash shrimps, butter and all of the seasons, 1/3 cup of water mix well

Allow to cook for 20 to 25 minutes or until shrimps are pink and tender.

Serve hot.

Fried Catfish, Whiting and Perch

Ingredient (100% homemade)

2 catfish, 2 whiting, 2 perch fillets, 2 cup of corn meal, 1 teaspoon of salt and pepper

2 cups of cooking oil

STEP 1:

Get a knife and run it on the outside of fish to make sure no scale is on fish.

STEP 2:

In a skillet add oil and turn skillet on medium high

STEP 3

Add salt and pepper to fish and place in corn meal

STEP 4:

Place fish in hot oil and cook until golden brown on both side.

Oven Lemon and Pepper Bake Fish

Ingredient (100% homemade)

3 to 5 whole fish fillet in half (tilapia or your favorite fish). 1 cup of lemon juice, 1 table spoon of garlic powder, 1 table spoon of black pepper, ½ cup of wine or beer,1/2 cup of water

STEP 1:

Wash fish and lay them out on a plate or pan and sprinkle all the dry season on front and back of the fish

STEP 2:

In a non-stick pan, pour the wine or beer ½ of the lemon juice. ½ cup of water in the pan

STEP 3:

Lay the fish flat in the pan add the rest of the lemon juice cover with foil for 10 minutes.

Finally put in oven on 325 and let cook for 10 minutes but check fish after 5 minutes to make sure that there is liquid in the bottom of pan if dry add ½ cup of water

Serve with rice, green beans (Serve Hot)

Meat loaf

Ingredient (100% homemade)

2 pound of hamburger meat, 1 can of ½ spaghetti sauce, ½ teaspoon of salt and pepper,1 egg 1- 6 oz can of vegetable soup,2 tablespoon of BBQ sauce, and 2 end slice of white or wheat bread crumbled.

STEP 1:

In a mixing bowl, add hamburger meat, salt, pepper, vegetable soup, 1 tablespoon of BBQ sauce, egg, the crumbled bread and 1/2 of spaghetti sauce mix well

STEP 2:

In a pan, put all of meat in it and shape as you desire a circle or a oval shape, but make sure it is even add the rest of the spaghetti and BBQ sauce on top. Spread even put in oven on 300 degree and cook for 25 to 30 minutes, drain the extra juice off and serve hot.

Collard Greens with Turkey Necks and Ham

Ingredient (100% homemade)

2 bunches of collard greens, 3 cap of oil, 2 cap vinegar, neck bones, ham hocks, or turkey necks, 2 tablespoon salt (You can buy the green already pick and cut up or you can buy) 1 to 2 bunches of green and you pick and cut them up that is the way I go) you will need a pot, knife and trash can take each leaf of green and look on both side for bugs etc..

Use your hand fold leaf in half and pull from the steam. Once you have done them all, put 4 to 5 leaf on top of each other, fold, use your knife, and cut into desire size such as 1/3 inch thick.

Once you have done that you will use both side of your sink with warm to hot water pour salt over the raw greens.

Put in a deep pot add ½ of the pot with water and add some smoke neck bones, or ham hocks or a pack of smoke turkey necks cook on medium heat.

Back to washing the greens. Make sure that your water changes from green to clear, but you do not add salt to make water change. Just warm water. Once the greens are clear, add to pot with meat in it and turn the pot on low until the green cook down.

Add salt, 3 cap full of vinegar and 3 caps of oil let cook for 2 to 3 hours.

Cabbage with Smoked Neckbones

Ingredient: (100% homemade)

A whole cabbage, 1 green bell pepper smoke neck bones, 1-teaspoon black pepper and ½ teaspoon of salt and 1 teaspoon of garlic powder

STEP 1:

Wash meat and put in a 3-quart pot add 2 cup of water alone with the garlic powder, pepper and salt (optional) let cook for 45 minute, pour 75% of the water out of the pot.

STEP 2:

Wash and cut the cabbage in half, you will now need a plate, alone with a slicing knife. Slice the leaves/ cabbage in 1/3 slices rinse and add to pot and the same for the green bell pepper (make sure you cut out the seeds in the bell pepper, you only want the green part of the bell pepper)

STEP 3:

Let cook for 10 minutes (you want the cabbage to have a little crunch to them but at the same time you want them to be tender).

Broccoli and Onions

Ingredient: (99% homemade)

(Using Frozen) you will need 2 bags of frozen broccoli 1 onion slice, 1 teaspoon of salt and pepper, 2 teaspoon of garlic and ½ cup of water.

Wash broccoli, put in a 3-quart pot with ½ cup of water, add salt (optional) pepper, garlic and ½ of the slice onion and add the broccoli

Let cook on medium heat for 15 minutes or until broccoli steam is tender.

Add the remaining of the slice onions and let cook for 5 to 10 addition minutes remember the broccoli must have a crunch but steam tender.

Sweet Candied Yams

Ingredient :(100% homemade)

20 whole sweet potatoes / cut in ½ quarter size 3 cups of sugar, 1 cup of 100% orange juice, 2 teaspoon of vanilla favor, 2 teaspoon of nutmeg, 2 tablespoon on cinnamon

STEP 1:

In a large pan, add cut sweet potatoes allow them to in the oven on 350 degrees until tender.

STEP 2:

Once tender add others ingredients

STEP 3:

Taste and see if sweet enough if not sweet enough, add more sugar by 1/2.cup you can always add flavor, nutmeg accord to your taste bud.

STEP 4:

Put pan in oven on 300 for 1 hour

Potatoes and Onions with sharp shredded Cheese

Ingredient (100% homemade)

1-5 pound bag of white potatoes, 1 medium onion cut in cubes, 1 cup of shred cheese of salt and black pepper, 1 stick of butter.

STEP 1:

Peel and wash cut potatoes; add all ingredients except the shredded cheese. (Set cheese aside) Put potatoes in medium pan and put in the oven on 350 degrees for 30 minutes. (Check the potatoes by sticking a folk in it, if the fork goes through it is done, or get a piece of potatoes if you can squeeze it then it is done.

STEP 2:

Once the potatoes are done, drain 75% of the water off and cover the potatoes with the cheese (You should only see the cheese, no potatoes on top, allow to go back in the oven until the cheese has melted completely) serve hot.

Southern Sweet Style fried Corn

Ingredient: (100% homemade)

10 to 12 ears of corn, ½ cup of flour,1 cup of sugar, 5 capful of oil, 1 teaspoon of black pepper, 1 ½ stick of butter.

Shuck the corn and clean all the string from around the corn. Take a sharp knife, go from top to bottom, and cut the corn off the cob place in a bowl.

In a skillet add the butter, corn, pepper in the oil let cook for 5 to 10 minutes on medium high.

Add the flour and the sugar .add ½ cup of water and cook for 20 minutes (Constance stir, put lid on and simmer for 10 minutes.

Macaroni and Cheese

Ingredient (100 % homemade)

1 16 oz box of Macaroni noodles, 4 cups of shred cheese, 4 cups of whole or 2% milk, 2 tablespoon of accent, 3 table spoon of self rising flour, 1 stick of melted butter, 1 teaspoon of salt, 2 teaspoon of pepper, 1 strainer 1 medium aluminum pan.

STEP 1:

In a medium pot add 1 teaspoon of salt allow the pot to boil for about 3 minutes, add ½ of the Macaroni noodles check for tenderness after 12 minutes if tender, drain and put in aluminum pan repeat with the other noodles in box

STEP 2:

Get another medium to large pot add melted butter, accent, stir, add self rising flour mix,add milk . You must continuously stir until mixture looks like a milk shake, then add melted cheese, salt and pepper, mix and pour into pan. Then add more shredded cheese and put in oven on 300 until cheese is melted (you know that it is done when the cheese melts and a golden brown ring is around the pan.

The mac n cheese should be ready in 20 minutes.

Red Beans and Rice

Ingredient: (50% homemade)

(The easy and simple receipt)

2 cans of red kidney beans, 2 bags of success rice (boil in a bag) 1/2 onion cut in cubes, 1 pinch of salt and pepper.

STEP 1:

In a 3-quart pot add the 2 bags of success rice with 2 cup of water and allow boiling for 15 minute.

STEP 2:

Once the rice get done add the kidney beans and onions, add the salt and pepper and allow to cook on medium heat for 10 minutes or until hot.

Black Eye Peas with Ham Hocks

Ingredient: (100% homemade)

1-pound bag of black eye peas, 6 ham hocks, 1 onion medium diced, 2 teaspoons of salt.

STEP 1:

In a medium pot, wash your ham hocks put in the pot with 3 cups of water, add onions, salt and pepper let cook for 30 minutes on medium.

STEP 2:

In a bowl use warm water add the dry black eye peas cover for 30 minutes,

STEP 3:

Once 30 minutes are up get the ones that do not look right out of bowl rinse the peas, put in the pot with the onion, and cook on medium heat for 30 to 45 minutes (you can tell when the peas are done because they will be tender).

Hopping John

Ingredient: (95% homemade use frozen/can peas)

1 bag of Success Rice (in the box), 2 cans of Black eye peas (n in the can), 1 can of stewed tomatoes, (onions and tomatoes are optional)

STEP 1:

Boil the rice in a 2 quart pot add 2 cup of water in pot

STEP 2:

Once the rice gets done (bag is filled/puff) drain and add black eye peas and ¼ can of the tomatoes, add a pinch of salt and pepper. Cook for 10 minutes and serve hot.

Butter Beans with Onions cook with fat back meat

Ingredient: (95 % using frozen vegetables)

1 pack of stew meat, ½ onion(cut in medium cubes),1/2 pound of butter beans, 1 teaspoon of pepper and salt (optional) 1 cup of water

STEP 1:

In a 3-quart pot add water and wash the fat back meat and add to the pot, add ½ of the onions and salt and pepper Cook on medium for 20 minutes.

STEP 2:

Add the frozen beans and the remaining of the onions and beans and let cook on medium for 20 minutes or until beans are tender.

Steam Squash and Onions

Ingredient: (100% homemade)

6 to 10 whole squashes slices (2 inch thick)
1 whole onion cut in cubes, 2 tablespoon of
garlic and herbs, 1 teaspoon of pepper and salt
(salt optional)

STEP 1:

In a 3-quart pot, add ½ Cup of water.

STEP 2:

Wash the slice squashes and put in pot add
ingredient. Let cook until tender.

Squash Casserole

Ingredient (100% homemade)

STEP 1:

8-10 squashes or 2 cans of slice squashes, ½ onion, Cook until done (if use cans warm them, Drain water, mash the squashes up, Add 4 eggs, 1 teaspoon tabasco sauces, 2 teaspoon parsley flakes add, Add 1 pinch of salt and 1 pinch of peppers, Butter your casserole dish and sat aside.

STEP 2:

Mix 2 cups of crumble crackers (saltine) and butter and spread in bottom of pan.

STEP 3:

Mix all ingredients spread all over #2 (squash mix in casserole pan add remaining of crumble crackers on top of mix.

STEP 4:

Place in oven on 350 and bake for 35 to 40 minutes or until golden brown.

Fried Squash

Ingredient: (100% homemade)

6 to 8 squashes slice,1 cup of self rising flour, 2 cup of oil, 1 egg beaten, ½ cup of milk, ½ teaspoon of pepper, ½ teaspoon of garlic, ½ teaspoon of salt (optional)

STEP 1:

Put oil in a 3-quart pot, allow the oil to get hot.

STEP 2:

Beat 1 egg and milk together.

STEP 3:

Add pepper, salt and garlic to washed squashes dip one at a time in the egg batter and then into the flour and put in hot oil, it is done, when they look golden.

Steam Rutabaga season with Fried Bacon

Ingredient: (95% homemade)

Use frozen rutabaga

2 rutabaga cut in cubes, 3 slice of bacon, 1/3 cup of water and ½ teaspoon of salt and pepper.

STEP 1:

Add the water to the 2-quart pot, wash the cubes rutabaga and place in pot alone with all the others ingredients.

STEP 2:

Let cook on medium heat until tender.

STEP 3:

Serve hot.

Fried Green Tomatoes

Ingredient (100% homemade)

4 mediums to large green and hard tomatoes, 1 cup of self-rising corn meal, 1 cup of self-rising flour, 1 cup of 2 % milk, 2 eggs, 2 cups of oil 1 tablespoon of garlic(optional), Tomatoes need to be green and hard.

STEP 1:

Wash and dry tomatoes, slice tomatoes 1/3-inch-thick (1tomatoe should give you 5 to 6 slices) or desire slices, sprinkle the garlic, (salt) pepper on both side

STEP 2:

(In another bowl add 2 eggs and 1/3 cup of milk) in another bowl have ½ of corn meal or self-rising flour

STEP 3:

(If you want the crunch add the corn meal if not add flour) first dip season tomato into egg batter then dredge into meal or flour batter, back into the egg batter. In the frying pan, add 1 cups of oil. Allow the frying pan to get hot and place the tomatoes in the hot oil and let cook on each side for 3 to 5 minutes or until golden brown.

STEP 4:

On a plate or rack place 4 folded paper towel place the hot tomatoes on it when done.

Bake Sweet Potato

Ingredient: (100% homemade)

5 to 6 sweet potatoes (medium) ½ stick of butter

Wash and poke holes in the potatoes put in oven until a folk can go all the way in them. Serve with butter.

Okra, Corn, and Tomatoes

Ingredient: (95% homemade) use canned

2 cans of whole corn, 2 can of cut up okra, 2 cans of stewed tomatoes, a pinch of salt and pepper and 1 teaspoon of garlic

STEP 1:

Mix all ingredient in a 3-quart pot and let cook on medium heat for 10 minutes Serve hot.

Deep-fried Okras

Ingredient (100% homemade)

20 okras (slice them in 1/3)

1 cup of oil, 1 cup of self- rising corn meal, 1 teaspoon of salt/pepper, 1 egg beaten, Garlic powder is optional

STEP 1:

Put oil in a 2-quart pot and allow oil to get hot.

STEP 2:

Mix and beat egg, with 1/3 cup of milk,

STEP 3:

Mix the okras with salt, pepper and garlic, dip in egg batter and then drop them in the hot oil.

The okras are done when they are light brown or golden

96

Stuffed Cheesy Potatoes

INGREDIENT (100% homemade)

10 whole white potatoes, Cheese hamburger meat, 2 teaspoon salt and pepper, and 2 Cups of shredded cheese

STEP 1:

Wash and place all potatoes in oven on 325degrees (it will be tender) you can stick a fork in it and the fork will go through when done

Place aside

STEP 2:

In another pot put hamburger meat, add salt, pepper stir when done drain add 1 cup of shredded cheese mix well.

STEP 3

Then split the potatoes in half, spoon out the center and place center of potatoes in another bowl spoon in the hamburger mix and put the potatoes back cover the top with shredded cheese put in oven for 10 minutes or until the top cheese has melted. Serve hot

Cracklin Cornbread

Ingredient: (100% homemade)

2 cups of self rising corn meal,1 cup of milk, 2 cup of sugar, ½ stick of butter,1/4 cup of cooking oil, 1 cup of fine chopped crackling, 1 egg

STEP 1:

Pour: the butter and oil in a cast iron /regular skillet put in oven on 300 degree allowing butter to melt

STEP 2:

In a mixing bowl, add the corn meal, sugar, milk, egg and the crackling mix

STEP 3:

Once the oil and butter melt pour 90 % into the batter and mix well once mix pour back into the hot pan and put in oven on 325 degree and allow it to cook until top is golden brown (15 minutes)

Cornbread Dressing

INGREDIENT: (100% homemade)

2 cups of self rising corn meal, ½ stick of butter melted, ½ cup of oil, 1 cup of sugar, 2 eggs, 1 cup of milk, 1 medium alumni pan, 1 teaspoon of nutmeg, 2 teaspoon of cinnamon, 2 can of chicken broth, 2 pack of season blend nutmeg, cinnamon, chicken broth and season

STEP 1:

Put butter and oil in pan put in oven on 300 (when hot remove from stove).

STEP 2:

In a medium bowl mix corn-meal, eggs, sugar, milk, and from the hot pan add ½ of the oil and butter into the mix, stir well and place in the alumni pan and place pan in oven for 20 minutes or until bread is golden brown

STEP 3:

Once bread is done in a medium pan crumbier bread add 1 teaspoon of nutmeg, 3 teaspoon of cinnamon, 2 can of chicken broth, 2 pack of season blend you may have to add 2 cups of water.

Put in oven for 30 minutes or until golden brown or around the edges is brown.

Cornbread Muffins

INGREDIENT: (100% homemade)

2 cups of self rising corn meal ½ stick of butter melted ½ cup of oil 1 cup of sugar, 2 eggs, 1 cup of milk, Cup cake pan,

STEP 1:

Put butter and oil in pan put in oven on 325 (when hot remove from stove).

STEP 2:

In a medium bowl mix corn meal, eggs, sugar, milk, and from the hot pan add ½ of the oil and butter into the mix. Stir well and place several spoons of batter into cupcake paper that sits in pan. Place pan in oven for 10-15 minutes or until bread is golden brown. Take one muffin out of it place and split to see if done or take a tooth pick and place in the center pull out if nothing is on the toothpick it is done. Remove pan and let cool for 5 minutes and put on plate, and do the same until all batter is gone.

Sweet Potatoes Bread

Ingredient: (100% homemade)

2 cup of self rising white corn meal, 1 cup of sugar, 1 egg,1 cup of milk, ½ stick of butter, 1/3cup of oil, 3 medium sweet potatoes or 2 cans of sweet potatoes.

STEP 1:

In a pan add the butter and oil and put in oven until hot and melted 300 degrees.

STEP 2:

(Using the cans) in a mixing bowl, mix the meal, sugar, egg, milk, and the canned sweet potatoes. Add melted butter and oil mixture in mix. Stir well and put in the hot pan. Put in oven for 30 minutes or until golden brown, if your mixture in pan is soupy then keep in oven for 10 to 15 more minutes.

Buttermilk/Regular or Cheese Biscuits

Ingredient: (100% homemade)

You can buy them from the freezer section in the grocery store already made.

1 cup flour,1 cup, Bisquick, 4 teaspoons, baking powder,1 tablespoon Sugar, ½ teaspoon, Salt, ¼ teaspoon, baking soda, 4 tablespoons,butter (room temperature), 1 cup milk

Preheat oven to 450 degrees.

STEP 1:

Add the flour, Bisquick, baking powder, sugar, salt, and baking soda to a large mixing bowl. Stir well to combine the dry ingredients thoroughly. Add two tablespoons of the butter to the dough and use a spoon to press it into the flour mixture. Once the first two tablespoons are completely incorporated, add in the last two tablespoons and repeat the process.

STEP 2:

Pour in the milk and stir with a spoon until just combined. The dough will likely be too wet. Add in more flour, one tablespoon at a time, until the dough is just dry enough to handle. Dough should come away clean from your fingers when you touch it but stick to your fingers if you pinch it. Dump dough onto a well-floured work surface. Sprinkle lightly with flour.

STEP 3:

Fold dough over 4 times, add 2 cup of shred cheese using your hands to shape dough, lay flour dough out on counter and using a coffee cup or a cookie cutter, cut the biscuits and place on a non- stick cooking sheet, let suit on counter for 10 minutes before placing in oven.

STEP 4:

The biscuits are done when the top is golden. Do not over cook. Let stand for 5 minutes before serving.

Sweet Potatoe Pie

INGREDIENT: (100% homemade)

6 Sweet potatoes, 1 cup milk, 3 eggs,3 tablespoon of cinnamon, 2 Tablespoon of nutmeg, 2 tablespoon of vanilla flavor ½ cup orange juice, 1 teaspoon of self rising flour, 3 cup of sugar, 4 pie shell

STEP 1:

Boil potatoes, once tender drain water and peel put peel potatoes in bowl add all ingredient mix well (sample a taste to see if it sweet enough if not add more sugar and flavor, and nutmeg

STEP 2:

Mix well and put into pie shell and put in oven on 350 degrees for 10 to 15 minutes or until golden brown.

Blackberry Slang/Cobblin

Ingredients: (95% homemade)

2 ½ cups fresh or frozen or can (thawed and drained) blackberries (do not use blueberries) 1cup sugar 1 cup all-purpose flour 2 teaspoons baking powder ½ teaspoon salt 1 ½ cup of milk

STEP 1:

1-cup milk in medium bowl, stir together blackberries and sugar. Let stand about 20 minutes or until fruit syrup forms. Heat oven to 375°F.

STEP 2:

In large bowl, stir together flour, baking powder, salt and milk. Stir in melted butter until blended. Spread in ungreased 8-inch square pan. Spoon blackberry mixture over batter.

STEP 3:

Bake 45 to 55 minutes or until dough rises and is golden.

Peach Cobbler

Ingredient: (10% homemade)

2 cans of peaches in it own juice.

4 Ready deep dish shell / pie crusts, ½ cup of sugar and 1 tablespoon of cinnamon, ½ teaspoon of nutmeg

STEP 1:

Open 3 cans of peaches in it own juice, mix the cinnamon nutmeg, and the sugar, pour into the ready deep dish pie shell/crust (take the other pie crust out of pan and put on top of the pie with the mixture fold and pinch the crust together . Take a knife and put 4 lines in the middle of the pie

STEP 2:

Cook on 350 degrees and when the crust is golden brown it is ready take out and let cool for 10 minutes before serving

Fried Apples

Ingredient: (100% Homemade)

Wash, peel and slice 6 whole apples in a 6 inch frying skillet, add ½ stick of butter, 1 teaspoon of lemon juice,1/4 cup of brown sugar but white sugar will do, 1 1/3 teaspoon of ground cinnamon,1/3 teaspoon of nutmeg, mix well, put lid on and cook on medium heat for 20 minutes .

Can be serve over Biscuits or Vanilla ice cream.

Apple Pie

Ingredient: 95% homemade (using caned apples) 2 cans of cooked apples in it own juice, 2 pack of Betty Crocker pie crust mix (in the box)

STEP 1:

PIE CRUST: Stir piecrust mix and cold water until pastry forms a ball, flatten ball into a round (2 rounds for two-crust pie) on floured surface. Roll ½ inches larger than upside-down 9-inch pie plate.

STEP 2:

Fold in half: place in pie pan, unfold and fit into pan, press firmly on the bottom and side.

STEP 3:

Put oven on 450 degrees bake for 8 to 10 minutes then ut in filling, crust on top, and put in oven for until golden brown.

Multiple colored Lemon Cupcakes with or without a Glaze

Ingredients: (100% homemade)

STEP 1:

Mix 1 cup salted butter softened 8 ounces cream cheese softened 2 cups sugar 6 large eggs 1/4 cup freshly squeezed lemon juice 1 tablespoon lemon zest 1 teaspoon lemon extract 1 teaspoon vanilla extract 3 cups all-purpose flour, 1 cupcake pan and cupcake liner.

STEP 2

Mix all ingredient mix well

STEP 3:

Place liner in cupcake pan, put mix evenly in the pan put oven on 325 degrees and cook for 20 minutes (place a toothpick in the center if nothing come out on it then they are done but if batter comes on it than cook for 10 more minutes and check again.

STEP 4:

Lemon Glaze 1 cup powdered sugar 2 tablespoons lemon juice 1/2 teaspoon vanilla extract

Tea Cakes

INGREDIENT: (100% homemade)

1/2 cup butter, softened 1 cup sugar 2 large eggs 2 1/2 cups all-purpose flour 2 teaspoons baking powder 1/2 teaspoon ground nutmeg 1 tablespoon milk.

STEP 1:

Beat butter at medium speed with an electric mixer until creamy; gradually add sugar, beating well. Add eggs, beating until blended.

STEP 2:

Combine flour, baking powder, and nutmeg; add to butter mixture alternately with milk, beginning and ending with flour mixture. Beat at low speed just until blended after each addition.

STEP 3:

Divide dough in half; cover with plastic wrap, and chill 1 hour.

STEP 4:

Roll half of dough to 1/4-inch thickness on a lightly floured surface. Cut with a 2 1/4-inch round cutter, and place on greased baking sheets. Repeat procedure with remaining half of dough.

STEP 5:

Bake at 350° for 8 minutes. (Cookies will be pale.) Cool on wire racks.

Rum Cake with Cream Cheese Icing

Ingredients: (0% Homemade)

Get 2 boxes of cake mix (of your choice)

½ pint of Dark Rum

Follow the instruction on the cake boxes, add rum mix well and put into a bunt pan.

Follow the cooking instruction, get a toothpick, insert into the cake if cake batter is on the toothpick then it needs to go back in oven for 10 minutes, recheck if nothing is on a clean toothpick then it is done.

Allow it to sit for 10 minutes before serving; Icing of your choice can be applied.

For 100% homemade e-mail me at cooking with Mrs.faye@protonmail.com

Butter Milk Sweet Corn Bread

Ingredients: 100%:

1 medium pan , 2 cups of self rising corn meal, ½ stick of butter , 1/3 cup of oil, 1 cup of sugar,, 1 egg, 1/2 cup of regular milk , 1 cup of cold butter milk.

STEP 1:

(Put oil and butter in the medium pan and put in oven on 300degrees until the butter melt)

In a medium mixing bowl mix all the ingredient, pour ½ of the oil and butter into the mixing bowl mix well

Pour the mixture into the pan and put in oven for 30 minutes

Stick a toothpick in 2 places, 1 being the center, and another places in the bread if nothing comes out on the tooth -pick then the bread is done

 While the bread is hot slice it and crumble in bowl pour the cold milk on top and eat and enjoy.

salt and mix on medium speed until fully combined.

Red Velvet Cake with and without Pecans

Ingredient: (100% homemade)

STEP 1:

2 ½ Cup plain flour, 1 ½ cup of sugar, 1 teaspoon of salt, 1 teaspoon of coco, shift flour sugar, salt add coco together

STEP 2:

In a different bowl: mix 1 cup of butter milk, 1 ½ cup Crisco oil, 2 eggs, 1 teaspoon vanilla flavor add 1 oz bottle of red food coloring blend all in cake mix

STEP 3:

Mix together 1 teaspoon of vinegar, 1-teaspoon baking soda, after mixing pour into the mix

STEP 4:

Pour into 9 inch blunt pan and place in over on 350 degree for 35 minutes (place a toothpick in the center if nothing comes on it then the cake is done, if batter on the toothpick then cook for 10 more minute.

Step 5: Frosting1-8 oz of cream cheese, 1 stick of butter,1 teaspoon of vanilla flavor,1 ½ box of confetti sugar (powder)add 1 cup of chop pecan on top of the cake when cold (optional).

Bread Pudding

INGREDIENTS: (100% homemade)

2 Cups of milk ¼ cup of, butter,2 eggs beaten,
½ cup sugar, 1 teaspoon of ground cinnamon, 1
teaspoon of nutmeg, 1/4 teaspoon salt 8 cups of
soft bread cut in cubes (about 8 slices of bread) ½
cup of raisins (optional)

STEP 1:

Heat oven to 350 degree Heat milk, butter
until warm Combine all ingredients together,
pour into an ungreased deep dish baking pan
bake uncover for 45 minutes.

Devil/Stuff Eggs

Ingredient: (100% homemade)

6 eggs, 1 tablespoon of mayo, 1 teaspoon of mustard, 3 tablespoon of pickle relish, 1 pinch of salt and pepper, Sprinkle pf paprika

STEP 1:

Put eggs in pot and add ½ teaspoon of salt (let boil for 10 minutes)

STEP 2:

Get 1 egg and run under cold water, take a butter knife and split egg in half (if egg is not running then it is done). Repeat until you have split and separate all eggs. Put the white part of the egg in a separate plate, yellow egg into a medium bowl crumble very fine and add mayo, mustard, sweet pickle relish salt and pepper mix well if there are your desired tasted sprinkle the paprika on them and refridgerator.

Apple, Raisin, Carrots, and Pineapple Salad

INGREDIENT: (100% homemade)

6 Raw carrots shredded, 4 Red Apple, 4 Green Apple, 1 Can of Tibbets Pineapples, 6 Boxes Raisins (SMALL) 12 Celery stalk cut in small cubes (optional).

STEP 1:

In a medium to large bowl cut all ingredient into medium cubies (the pineapples are already cut just open the can and pour off the juice drain and put into bowl add 4 tablespoon of mayonnaise (if the mixture is too dry add more mayo.

134

Chicken Salad

Ingredient: (95% homemade)

1 pound box of macaroni noodles, 2 cans of (chicken in a can) ½ jar of pickled relish, ½ cup of mayonnaise and mustard, ½ teaspoon of pepper and salt (optional).

STEP 1:

Cook the macaroni noodles (They are done when tender. Once done add all of ingredient little at a time. (If too dry add more mustard and mayno, onions cubes can be added. Serve Cold with Crackers.

Tuna Salad

Ingredient: (100% homemade)

2 cans of tuna in water or oil,1 16 oz box of Macaroni noodles, 1/2 cup of mayonnaise, 2 tablespoon of mustard, ½ teaspoon of salt and black pepper, onions (optional) 2 cups of water 3 tablespoon of sweet pickles relish.

STEP 1:

In a 2 quart pot add 2 cups of water bring to a boil, add Macaroni noodles allow to cook until they are tender once tender run cold water on them sat aside in a medium bowl open and drain the tuna, put in bowl add 2 tablespoons of mayonnaise, mustard, and add pickle relish .

STEP 2:

Add Cooked Macaroni Noodles in with the tuna mix well if you need too add more mustard and mayonnaise, now you can, add onions if desire serve cold.

Potato Salad

Ingredients: (100% homemade)

1 onion, bell pepper dice small, 5 lb white potatoes, 3 tablespoon pickle relish, 3 tablespoons of mayonnaise mustard (yellow mustard) 1 teaspoon of salt and pepper, 4 eggs

Peel and cut your potatoes in 1/3 in cubes. Wash and put in medium pot add the 4 eggs in the water let boil for 20 minutes. Once the potatoes boil (you can stick a fork in them if the fork goes all the way in, they are done. Drain and place potatoes in a mixing bowl, add the pickle relish, mustard, mayo, salt, pepper, onion and bell peppers.

Spread salad even in the bowl slice the eggs and place around the bowl add paprika.

Pasta Salad

Ingredient: (100% homemade)

2 -12 oz box of bow tie noodles,1 medium sweet onion thin slice, 2 cucumbers thin sliced, 1 block of sharp cheddar cheese cut in 1 inch cubes, 2 pint of cherries tomatoes if you leave them whole but if you cut in half use only 1 pint, 2 bottle of zesty Italian dressing.

STEP 1:

Cook noodles in a 2 quart pot when tender drain and rinse with cold water add all ingredients mix well and place in ice box until ready to serve (if dry add more dressing)

Cole Slaw

INGREDIENT: (100% homemade)

1 bag of Cole slaw mix 1 green pepper slices 2 sweet onions slice (thin) 2 ¾ cup of sugar 2¾ cup of Hines white vinegar 1 ½ cup of cooking oil 1tablespoon regular yellow mustard ½ teaspoon of salt 1 teaspoons of black pepper

STEP 1:

Mix sugar, oil, vinegar, mustard, stir well and put on medium to high burner and boil for 3 to 7. While boiling, in a big bowl with lid open, add slaw mix and pour into bowl add celery seed and (salt is optional), black pepper, bell peppers and onions. Pour the hot mixture over the slaw mix.

Stir well, put a lid on it, put into the refrigerator, and stir every 4 to 6 hours for a 24-hour period, serve cold.

Faye's Garden Toss Salad

Ingredients: (100% homemade)

Lettuce, tomatoes, cucumbers, bell peppers, onions, pineapples, dried cranberries, boil eggs, honey pecan, walnuts, tortilla chips, pepperoni, turkey slice, chicken nuggets, carrots, raw broccoli, raw cauliflower, cheese and dressing

(All vegetables are slice thin, lettuce is slice into ¾, inch, eggs are cut into squares walnuts and pecans, and chips are cumbered, all meats are cut into chunks)

In a 9 inch serving plate place as followed:

Lettuce, cucumbers, bell peppers, carrots, broccoli, cauliflower, onions, pepperoni, chicken nuggets, pineapples, dried cranberries, boil eggs, turkey slice, walnuts and pecans, tomatoes and tortilla chips and cheese and your favorite dressing

Fruit Salad in a Cantaloupe Shell

In a cantaloupe shell add no seed watermelon, cantaloupe, pineapples, grapes, blueberries, peaches if desire .place in icebox for 15 minutes before serving.

ACKNOWLEDGMENTS

I give all praise, thanks and glory to my Father in Heaven, for allowing and creating my mind, the knowledge and the know how to make this book possible. To Aunt Martha (Mot) and Bessie Mae thanks for the love and for answering the thousands of questions that I had about certain dishes and the ingredients that your mother and my Grannie prepared.

A special thanks to my best friend who listen, correct me when I am wrong and still praise me when I am doing well. She is my stabilizing force. Ms. Loretta Rusley my Mother when God create her, he truly broke the mold, Mom I will always Love you and cherish your input.

To the Love of my life Mr. Willie J. Reese who has been in my life for 44 years and still counting. Honey thank you for being an inspirational and your encouragement. Your support, understanding and love is so Godley and appreciated.

I would like to thank our 4 adult children LaQuanda, Martharia, Willie Jr, (Serita), BerNard and our 15 Grandchildren for the support and leaving me alone during my writing time. I want you all to know that you are jewels and I appreciation each and every one of you.

Follow me at www.cookingwithmrsfaye.com

ABOUT THE AUTHOR

Mrs. Brenda Rusley Reese was born in Montgomery Alabama on December 27th 1960. She did not play outside often as a child; however, she did enjoy staying in the kitchen with her grandmother Annie Mae Rusley. At the age of five, her grandmother started teaching her how to cook everything from scratch/ homemade. While in high school, at the age of 14, she meet her high school love, Willie J. Reese, and Married him on February 3, 1981. Together they have 4 children and 15 grandchildren and now they reside in North Carolina. You can reach Brenda at cookingwithmrsfaye1@protonmail.com

Allow 6 to 24 hours for a respond, due to a high demand for 100% homemade recipes.

Printed in the United States
By Bookmasters